The Best Gluten-Free Dinner Cookbook

Amazingly Delicious Gluten-Free Dinner Recipes

BY: Ivy Hope

Copyright/License Page

Table of Contents

Introduction

The Gluten-Free Diet is a lifestyle that millions of people have adopted in order to live healthier lives. When our bodies can't process gluten - a protein found in wheat, barley and rye, everything from headaches to lethargy, depression, and even infertility can occur.

We are living in a time where gluten-free is becoming more popular than ever. People are now trying this diet even if they don't have any known allergies or intolerances to gluten. This is because they have learned about the health benefits that come along with the diet.

The recipes in this cookbook were created to help people on a gluten-free diet enjoy delicious and nutritious meals that they can share with their friends and family. One of the hardest things about adapting to a new diet is not being able to enjoy many of your old favorite meals.

The book is full of hearty dinners for your evenings, finger foods for social events, and desserts for your sweet tooth. It provides you with 50 gluten-free dinner recipes, each with a description and a picture.

The ingredients used in the recipes are easily available at your local grocery store or at any health food store. The directions are also easy to follow.

Happy cooking!

1. Quinoa Citrus Salad

A summer potluck favorite! This delicious grain salad is bursting with flavor from the fresh citrus fruits. Change it up by topping with chopped pecans or your favorite fish fillet.

Serving size: 4

Cooking time: 15 minutes

Ingredients:

- ½ cup quinoa
- 1 cup water
- ¼ cup orange juice
- 4 teaspoons freshly squeezed lime juice
- 3 tablespoons avocado oil
- ½ teaspoon chili powder
- ½ teaspoon salt (preferably pink Himalayan)
- ¼ teaspoon freshly ground black pepper
- 1 (10-ounce) bag baby arugula
- 1 navel orange, peeled and diced
- 1 red grapefruit, peeled and cut into sections
- 1 avocado, peeled, pitted, and cut into 1-inch pieces
- ½ cup almond slices

Instructions:

In a medium saucepan, combine the quinoa and water and cook according to package directions.

Meanwhile, in a small bowl, whisk together the orange juice, lime juice, oil, chili powder, salt, and pepper.

On four plates, evenly divide the arugula, quinoa, orange, grapefruit, avocado, and almonds.

Drizzle with the dressing and serve immediately.

2. Hearty Vegetable Soup

This hearty vegetable soup is a hearty and wholesome meal that is both healthy and delicious. The vegetables in this soup provide you with vitamins, minerals, and antioxidants that contribute to better health. It makes a quick and easy dish for busy weeknights.

Serving size: 4

Cooking time: 20 minutes

Ingredients:

- 1 (26-ounce) carton or can diced tomatoes, undrained
- 1 (16-ounce) bag frozen mixed vegetables (green beans, corn, peas, and carrots)
- 3 cups vegetable broth, divided
- Juice of 1 lemon
- 1 diced celery stalk
- ½ diced onion
- ½ cup chopped fresh parsley
- 2 teaspoons ground cumin
- 1 bay leaf
- ¼ teaspoon black pepper, freshly ground
- ½ teaspoon salt

Instructions:

In a large saucepan, combine the tomatoes, vegetables, 2 cups of broth, lemon juice, celery, onion, parsley, cumin, salt, bay leaf, and pepper.

Cover and cook over high heat until the edges of the soup start to bubble.

Reduce the heat to medium-low, cover, and simmer for 20 minutes, or until all the vegetables are soft, adding more of the broth if a thinner soup is desired.

3. Greek Chicken Casserole

This Greek Chicken Casserole is a whole lot of flavors and textures in one delicious dish! The ingredients in this dish meld together to create a satisfying, modern take on the traditional casserole. This casserole has all the amazing flavors of Cypriot cuisine: olives, capers, and lemon peel. It's perfect for weeknights when you don't have time to cook!

Serving size: 6

Cooking time: 45 minutes

Ingredients:

- 4 skinless, boneless chicken breast halves or 8 tights
- 2 pounds potatoes, cubed
- 1 pound green beans, trimmed and cut in 1-inch pieces
- 1 big onion, chopped
- 1 cup diced tomatoes
- 5 cloves garlic, minced
- 1/4 cup water
- ½ cup crumbled feta cheese
- salt and black pepper

Instructions:

Preheat oven to 350 F. Heat oil in a large baking dish over medium heat. Add onion and sauté for 2 minutes. Add thyme, black pepper, and garlic and sauté for another minute. Add potatoes and sauté, for 2-3 minutes, or until they begin to brown. Stir in beans, water, and tomatoes.

Remove them from the heat. Arrange chicken pieces into the vegetables, sprinkle with salt and pepper, and top with feta. Cover and bake for 40 minutes, stirring gently halfway through.

Serve the vegetable mixture on a plate underneath or beside the chicken.

4. Ground Beef and Rice Stuffed Peppers

Savor the deep savory flavors of these spiced ground beef and rice stuffed peppers. This dish is a healthy and easy-to-make family favorite with a mix of spices, rice, and ground beef. The sweet, slightly sour taste makes it a great way to spice up your meal rotation.

Serving size: 6

Cooking time: 48 minutes

Ingredients:

- 6 red or green bell peppers, cored and seeded
- 1 pound ground beef
- 1/4 cup rice, washed and drained
- 1 onion, finely cut
- 1 small tomato, grated
- a bunch of freshly chopped parsley
- 3 tablespoons olive oil
- 1 tablespoon paprika
- Salt and black pepper, to taste

Instructions:

Heat the oil and gently sauté the onion for 2-3 minutes. Remove from heat. Add paprika, ground beef, rice, and grated tomato, and season with pepper and

Combine ingredients very well and stuff each pepper with the mixture using a spoon. Every pepper should be 3/4 full.

Arrange the peppers in a deep ovenproof dish and top up with warm water to half fill the dish. Cover with a lid or foil and bake for about 40 minutes at 350 F. Uncover and bake for 5 minutes more.

Serve with yogurt and top with parsley.

5. Mediterranean Lamb Casserole

Mediterranean Lamb Casserole is a delicious, easy-to-make, and impressive dish that takes lamb from the ground to the table in a flash. The meat is cooked with Greek flavors, which include cumin, oregano, and cinnamon. In addition to being an exquisite main course for dinner or a party dish for your next event, this preparation is also good for leftovers because it's so flavorful.

Serving size: 5

Cooking time: 2 hours 27 minutes

Ingredients:

- 2 pounds boned lean shoulder of lamb
- 3 onions, sliced
- 2 garlic cloves, chopped
- 1 (15-ounce) can chickpeas, drained and rinsed
- 2 zucchinis, peeled and cubed
- 1 cup cherry tomatoes, halved
- 1 cup beef broth
- 1 cup tomato juice
- 3 tablespoons olive oil
- 1 tablespoon fresh rosemary, chopped
- 1 tablespoon fresh basil, chopped
- ½ teaspoon black pepper
- ½ cup fresh parsley leaves, to serve

Instructions:

Cut the lamb into 1-inch cubes. In an ovenproof casserole, heat 2 tablespoons of olive oil and gently sauté onions and garlic for about 2-3 minutes. Add the lamb and sauté, stirring, for about 4 minutes or until well browned on all sides.

Add in rosemary, tomato juice, and beef broth and bake in a preheated to 350 F for 1 hour.

Stir in the chickpeas and bake for a further 1 hour or until the lamb is almost tender. Stir in zucchinis, tomatoes, black pepper, and basil. Cook for about 20 minutes longer or until the lamb is tender.

Serve sprinkled with parsley.

6. Pork Roast and Cabbage

This dish is really so simple to make, and the ingredients are all relatively inexpensive. The only tricky part is trying to fit it all in one pot.

Serving size: 4

Cooking time: 30 minutes

Ingredients:

- 2 cups of cooked pork roast, chopped
- 1/2 head of cabbage, chopped
- 2 onions, chopped
- 1 lemon, juice only
- 1 tomato, chopped
- 1 teaspoon paprika
- 1/2 teaspoon cumin
- black pepper, to taste
- 2 tablespoons olive oil

Instructions:

Heat olive oil in an ovenproof casserole and sauté cabbage, pork and onions.

Add cumin, paprika, lemon juice, tomato, black pepper and stir. Cover and bake at 350 F until vegetables are tender.

7. Cabbage and Rice Stew

The flavors of cabbages and rice blend together to create a hearty, healthy dish. This is the best kind of comfort food. It is hearty, warming, and so easy to make! You can also use white or brown rice, as well as different vegetables. Also, this stew will freeze beautifully, so you can have it on hand for those busy days. Much like you probably do already.

Serving size: 4

Cooking time: 30 minutes

Ingredients:

- 1 cup long-grain white rice
- 2 cups water
- 2 tablespoons olive oil
- 1 small onion, chopped
- 1 clove garlic, crushed
- ½ head cabbage, cored and shredded
- 2 tomatoes, diced
- 1 tablespoon paprika
- 1 teaspoon cumin
- salt, to taste
- Black pepper, to taste
- ½ bunch of parsley, finely cut

Instructions:

Heat the olive oil in a large ovenproof casserole. Add in onion and garlic and cook until transparent. Add paprika, cumin, rice, and water, then stir and bring to a boil.

Simmer for 10 minutes. Add the shredded cabbage; tomatoes, and bake in a preheated to 350 F oven for about 20 minutes, occasionally stirring, until the cabbage cooks down.

Season with salt and pepper and serve sprinkled with fresh parsley.

8. Rice with Leeks and Olives

This is a simple rice dish with leeks, olives, and goat cheese. This is the perfect one-pot meal for dinner on a busy weeknight.

Serving size: 6

Cooking time: 25 minutes

Ingredients:

- 6 large leeks, cleaned and sliced into bite-sized pieces
- 1 large onion, chopped
- 20 black olives, pitted, chopped
- ½ cup hot water
- 5 tablespoons olive oil
- 1 cup rice
- 2 cups boiling water
- Freshly-ground black pepper, to taste

Instructions:

In a large casserole, sauté the leeks and onion in olive oil for 4-5 minutes. Add in the olives, rice, and boiling water; season with salt and black pepper.

Stir to combine and bake in a preheated to 350 F oven for 20 minutes.

9. Gluten-Free Artichoke and White Bean Stew

It's the perfect winter comfort food warming and hearty with fiber to fill you up. This Stew is hearty, flavorful, and, the best part, gluten-free! It's also vegan and healthy enough for anyone following a paleo diet. So whether you're looking for a healthy dinner or an indulgent treat, this dish has it all.

Serving size: 5

Cooking time: 20 minutes

Ingredients:

- 15 ounces artichoke hearts
- ½ bunch of kale
- 2 cups vegetable broth
- 1 tablespoon of dried basil
- 1 tablespoon of dried oregano
- 1 teaspoon of salt
- ½ teaspoon of red pepper flakes
- 28 ounces diced tomatoes, fire-roasted
- 15 ounces white beans
- Ground black pepper to taste

Instructions:

Prepare the vegetables. Unload the artichokes from the can and cut them into bite-size chunks. Remove stems and rinse the kale, then slice into ribbons. Diced the fire-roasted tomatoes. Set it aside and keep the liquid from the tomatoes.

In a deep pot, combine all spices with the vegetable broth and bring it to a boil.

Add the kale, artichokes, white beans, and tomatoes, including its liquid, in the deep pot. Let it boil over medium heat.

Set to low heat, then simmer for 20 minutes, stirring occasionally.

Best served hot.

10. Gluten-Free Sweet Potato Vegan Hash

This recipe is for all of you who are vegan or gluten-free and would rather eat something that tastes good than something that just tastes healthy. It is also for everyone else who prefers whole foods made with natural ingredients.

Serving size: 6

Cooking time: 20 minutes

Ingredients:

- 1 thinly sliced yellow onion
- 2 tablespoons of coconut oil
- 2 minced cloves garlic
- 3 large-size sweet potatoes, peeled and diced into half-inch cubes
- 12 ounces vegan chorizo
- 2 teaspoons of chili powder
- salt and ground pepper to taste
- 2 large handfuls of spinach
- 1 teaspoon peppermint extract

Instructions:

Boil water in a medium pot. Add cubed sweet potatoes and boil them for 5 minutes. Drain and set aside.

Set on medium heat and add oil in a heated skillet. Sauté onions for 5 minutes or until it turns fragrant and golden brown. Add the garlic and sauté for another minute more.

Toss in the drained sweet potatoes and sauté with the onion and garlic for 5 minutes or until the sweet potatoes turn soft.

Add the vegan chorizo, spinach, chili peppers, peppermint extract, salt, and pepper. Cook until the spinach wilts and the chorizo warm through.

Transfer to a serving dish immediately and serve.

11. Garlic Butter Noodles

Garlic butter noodles is a delicious and simple meal that you can make in the oven, on the stovetop, or even on top of your stove. This recipe is great for those cold winter nights - easy to make and sure to be a family favorite.

Serving size: 4

Cooking time: 5 minutes

Ingredients:

- 1 tablespoon olive oil
- ¼ cup minced garlic
- 8 tablespoons unsalted butter
- ½ teaspoon salt
- ½ teaspoon black pepper, freshly ground
- 4 cups cooked gluten-free pasta of your choice
- 1 cup grated Parmesan cheese

Instructions:

In a medium pan, heat the olive oil over medium heat. Add the garlic and cook it for 2 minutes.

Add the butter and let it melt. Add the salt and pepper.

Fold in the pasta, stirring until it's covered in sauce.

Put some Parmesan cheese and serve immediately.

12. Vegetable Fried Rice

This is a dish everyone loves! It's a spicy and fragrant rice that combines egg, chicken, and vegetables to create a complete meal. It's delicious as is or with some ketchup or hot sauce on top.

Serving size: 8

Cooking time: 10 minutes

Ingredients:

- 1 teaspoon olive oil
- 1 small onion, chopped
- 2 cups chopped carrots
- 2 cups frozen peas
- ½ teaspoon ground ginger
- 1 teaspoon garlic powder
- ½ teaspoon salt
- 3 large eggs
- 2 cups hot cooked brown rice
- ¼ cup gluten-free soy sauce
- 2 tablespoons unsalted butter

Instructions:

In a large pan, warm the olive oil over medium heat. Add the onion and carrots and sauté until the onion is translucent about 5 minutes.

Add the peas, ginger, garlic powder, and salt. Push the vegetables to one side of the pan.

In a small bowl, whisk together the eggs, then pour them into the open side of the pan.

Scramble the eggs and cook for 3 to 4 minutes. Stir the scrambled eggs into the veggies.

Add the rice, soy sauce, and butter.

Stir-fry for 1 minute to allow the butter to melt. Remove from the heat and serve.

13. Chickpea Curry with Kale

This curry is a vegetarian dish that is traditionally served on curries but can also be served as a vegetarian main course. It's an easy yet satisfying meal for any day of the week. I hope you enjoy it!

If you're looking for an easy weeknight dinner, this chickpea curry is just what your dinner menu needs! This recipe combines the rich flavors of Indian cuisine with the nutrient-packed ingredients that are so often found in vegan dishes.

Serving size: 4

Cooking time: 25 minutes

Ingredients:

For the spice blend

- 1 teaspoon ground cumin
- 1 teaspoon ground turmeric
- 1 teaspoon ground coriander
- 1 teaspoon sea salt
- ½ teaspoon cayenne pepper

For the curry

- 1 teaspoon coconut oil
- 1 small red onion, finely chopped
- 1 medium sweet potato, diced
- 2 garlic cloves, minced
- 1-inch piece fresh ginger, peeled and minced
- 1 (8-ounce) can diced tomatoes
- ½ cup vegetable stock or water
- ½ cup full-fat coconut cream, separated from the coconut milk
- 2 cans chickpeas
- 3 cups stemmed and chopped fresh kale

Instructions:

To make the spice blend

Put the cumin, turmeric, coriander, salt, and cayenne pepper. Mix well in a small pan.

To make the curry

Warm the oil within medium heat.

Put the onion, then cook for 2 to 3 minutes, or until fragrant and translucent.

Stir in the sweet potato and cook for another 2 minutes.

Add the garlic, ginger, and spice blend, and cook for another 30 seconds.

Put the tomatoes with their juices, stock, and coconut cream, then stir to combine.

Cover and cook over high heat, bringing the curry to a low boil. Add the chickpeas, then reduce the heat to low and simmer for about 20 minutes, or until the sweet potato is tender.

Remove, then stir in the kale before serving.

14. Portobello Mushroom Pizza

What's not to love about a Portobello Mushroom Pizza? It's got all the flavors of a traditional pizza with all the nutrients of a Portobello mushroom. In fact, this vegan pizza has an impressive amount of protein and fiber for such a small dish.

Serving size: 4

Cooking time: 10 minutes

Ingredients:

- 4 Portobello mushroom caps
- ¼ cup marinara sauce, divided
- 4 dashes Italian seasoning, divided
- 1 cup shredded mozzarella cheese, divided

Instructions:

Preheat the oven to 400°F.

Place the mushroom caps top down on a sheet pan lined with parchment paper.

Top each mushroom cap with marinara sauce.

Top each cap with a dash of Italian seasoning.

Sprinkle shredded mozzarella cheese evenly over each cap.

Bake for about 10 minutes, or until the cheese is melted and bubbling.

Allow to cool for 5 minutes before serving.

15. Black Bean Plantain Burgers

The best thing about plantains is that they can be eaten raw, cooked, or even ground into flour. This versatile fruit provides many cooking options while providing a healthy boost of vitamins and minerals. Another great thing about plantains is that they are relatively inexpensive for what you get out of them. With their versatility and ease of use, this fruit might be the best food to cook up to impress company.

Serving size: 8

Cooking time: 45 minutes

Ingredients:

- 1 medium plantain
- Salt
- 1 cup cooked black beans
- ½ medium red bell pepper
- ½ medium green bell pepper
- 4 cloves garlic
- 2 small tomatillos
- 2 chipotles in adobo
- ¼ teaspoon ground cumin
- ¼ teaspoon dried oregano
- ½ cup crushed tortilla chips
- Olive oil

Topping

- 1½ avocados
- ½ mango, cut into small chunks
- 1 teaspoon freshly squeezed lime juice
- Salt

Instructions:

Place the plantain pieces in a medium pot, then cover with water and salt. Boil. Decrease the heat, simmer and cook for 20-25 minutes; drain and let it cool.

Put in a food processor, then pulse it a few times. Put the rest of the burger fixing, except the crushed tortilla chips. Pulse until the chunky paste forms. Scoop into a large bowl and mix in the tortilla chips. For pan-fried burgers, warm a large pan within medium-low heat. Grease the pan with oil and cook for about 20 minutes per side.

Meanwhile, arrange the topping. Slice the avocado in half and exclude the pit. Scoop the flesh with a spoon—place it in a bowl. Put the mango. Mix in the lime juice, then season to taste with salt.

Serve the burgers with the avocado topping.

16. Coconut Curry Stuffed Sweet Potatoes

Using these ingredients, you can make a vegan but delicious meal to serve for dinner tonight! These crispy and creamy vegan stuffed sweet potatoes are baked to perfection in the oven, making them super easy yet super satisfying. For a healthy and flavorful twist on your favorite comfort food, try this simple recipe! If you're craving the flavors of a traditional curry dish but don't want to go through the hassle of making one from scratch, look no further.

Serving size: 6

Cooking time: 1 hour 20 minutes

Ingredients:

- 3 medium sweet potatoes
- Olive oil
- 3-4 teaspoons ginger
- 2-3 cloves garlic, minced
- ½ jalapeño pepper, minced
- ½ teaspoon dry mustard powder
- ¼ teaspoon ground turmeric
- ¼ teaspoon ground cumin
- ¼ teaspoon ground coriander
- ¼ teaspoon ground cinnamon
- Pinch crushed cardamom seeds
- 2 cups de-stemmed chopped kale
- ½ cup full-fat canned coconut milk

Instructions:

Clean the outside of the sweet potatoes to remove any dirt. Pat dry. Poke each potato using a fork a few times, then grease with oil. Put the potatoes on the middle or top rack in the oven and bake until cooked through about 1 hour. Remove, but leave the oven on.

Meanwhile, warm a medium pan within medium heat. Grease the pan with oil. Put the ginger, garlic, jalapeño, and spices. Warm until fragrant, about 1 minute. Put the kale, cook for 4-5 minutes.

Cut the potatoes in half alongside, then scoop the flesh.

Mash the scooped-out potato with the coconut milk in a bowl. Mix in the kale.

Scoop the potato/kale batter back into the potato halves.

Put the potato halves in a roasting pan and return to the oven to bake for another 15 minutes.

Chicken With Mashed Potatoes

17. The best meal we've ever had, and it was so easy!

It's just chicken and mashed potatoes. Really. Though we all know that this combination of starches and protein is a classic, and for a good reason. This dish is hearty, comforting, and delicious.

Serving size: 4

Cooking time: 20 minutes

Ingredients:

- 4 skinless, boneless chicken breasts
- 2 tablespoons extra virgin olive oil, divided
- 1½ cups unsalted chicken stock
- 2 skin-removed large potatoes
- ½ cup lactose-free milk
- 1 teaspoon black pepper, divided
- ¼ teaspoon salt, divided
- ¼ teaspoon turmeric
- 1 tablespoon minced parsley

Instructions:

High-heat 2 tablespoons of extra virgin olive oil in a pan. Add your chicken breast with salt, pepper, and turmeric and let it cook until golden brown on both sides. Add the chicken stock and cook for 5 minutes.

Cook all potatoes in a medium pot with a little pinch of turmeric.

Mash your potatoes and add the rest of salt and pepper.

Heat lactose-free milk in the microwave and add to your mashed potato. Whisk well.

Pour your plate with mashed potato and chicken on top. Sprinkle parsley on top.

18. Chicken Kebab

If you're looking for a new, easy to prepare meal for your family, think about making chicken kebabs! Unlike many other dishes, this one is easy to make and can be customized to suit your family's taste buds. Chicken kebabs are also very healthy because they are grilled or cooked on the stove instead of fried or baked.

Serving size: 4

Cooking time: 25 minutes

Ingredients:

- 4 chicken breasts, cut into 1.5 inches
- ¾ cup lactose-free yogurt or plain yogurt
- 1 large onion
- ¼ cup saffron (bloomed)
- 1 tablespoon salt
- 3 tablespoons extra virgin olive oil
- 1 tablespoon lemon juice

Instructions:

Cut your onions and make onion rings.

To marinate your chicken, mix and stir it well with onion, lactose-free plain yogurt, bloomed saffron, olive oil, salt, and lemon juice together (To have a bloomed saffron, you need to grind your saffron perfectly and add 100ml of boiling water to it).

Cover the marinated bowl and put it in the fridge to rest for two hours.

After two hours, thread the chickens into skewers and grill both sides well until golden brown.

19. Chicken Pizza

Chicken pizza is easy to make and so yummy, good for those cold nights together with your family. Try it out today.

Serving size: 4

Cooking time: 10 minutes

Ingredients:

- 4 gluten-free pizza crusts
- 1 cup sliced no-fat cooked chicken breast
- 1 cup shredded mozzarella or lactose-free cheese
- 4 tablespoons organic mayonnaise
- 1 teaspoon oregano powder

Instructions:

Place your gluten-free pizza crusts on a non-stick pizza pan or bake sheet.

Spread your organic low-fat, low-sodium mayo on your crust.

Add your cooked chicken breasts to your pizza.

Sprinkle with mozzarella or lactose-free cheese and oregano powder.

Let it bake at 480 °F for 10 minutes. Then, broil on the same heat for five more minutes until cheese is melted.

20. Turkey Zucchini Noodles

This is a zucchini noodle recipe that is so simple and quick to make, and you can probably whip it up in less than 10 minutes. It's also a healthy and delicious dish that you can enjoy for dinner. They're easy to cook, full of nutrients, and they taste great served with any type of sauce!

Serving size: 4

Cooking time: 10 minutes

Ingredients:

- 3 medium-size spiralized zucchinis or zucchini strips
- 1 pound skinless fat-free cooked turkey breasts
- 1 tablespoon extra-virgin olive oil, divided
- 2 cups of water
- ½ teaspoon turmeric
- ½ teaspoon salt
- 1 tablespoon tomato paste
- ¼ teaspoon stevia

Instructions:

Cook zucchini noodles in boiling water for 5 minutes.

Bring them out of the water and let them dry.

Heat your cooked turkey in a pan with extra virgin olive oil. Add turmeric, tomato paste, stevia, salt, and little water (100ml) for 5 minutes until golden brown on both sides.

Add your zucchini to your turkey and stir well. Enjoy!

21. Spaghetti & 'Meatballs'

Spaghetti and meatballs are an Italian meal that has become popular around the world. The dish consists of spaghetti noodles with sauce, Italian sausage, and mozzarella cheese. You can also add other toppings like bell peppers, olives, or mushrooms to make it more of a meal.

Serving size: 12

Cooking time: 25 minutes

Ingredients:

- 1 (18-ounce) can chickpeas, drained and rinsed
- 3 garlic cloves
- ½ cup gluten-free oats
- 1 teaspoon dried basil
- 1 teaspoon dried parsley
- 1 ½ teaspoons Dried oregano
- ½ teaspoon coarse salt
- ½ teaspoon black pepper
- 2 heaped tablespoons nutritional yeast
- ½ lemon, juiced
- 1 large zucchini, washed and grated
- 32 oz / 900 ml tomato or marinara sauce
- 8 oz / 225g gluten-free spaghetti

Instructions:

Place chickpeas, garlic, and oats in a food processor and pulse until finely chopped. Transfer to a large bowl and add all the herbs, seasoning, nutritional yeast, lemon juice, and zucchini and mix until well combined.

Scoop out a tablespoon of the mixture and roll into a ball, then place on the tray. Repeat until you have made 12 'meatballs. Bake in the oven within 25 minutes, flipping them over to cook evenly after 15 minutes of cooking.

While the 'meatballs' are cooking, cook the spaghetti according to packet directions and heat the marinara sauce gently over low heat. Combine the sauce with the pasta once both are cooked.

Serve the 'meatballs' on top of the marinara pasta while hot.

22. Cauliflower Tikka Masala

There is nothing more comforting in the winter months than a hearty, satisfying bowl of this simple, spicy recipe. Try it with garam masala for a spicy twist!

Serving size: 4

Cooking time: 25 minutes

Ingredients:

For the Curry:

- 1 tablespoon cooking oil
- ½ teaspoon mustard seeds
- ½ teaspoon cumin seeds
- 1 small onion, chopped
- 4 large cloves garlic, crushed
- 1 tablespoon ginger, finely grated
- ¾ teaspoon garam masala
- ½ teaspoon ground coriander
- ¼ teaspoon turmeric
- ½ teaspoon salt
- ½ teaspoon black pepper
- ½ teaspoon chili powder or red chili flakes
- 1 medium cauliflower

For the Sauce:

- 3 medium tomatoes, halved
- 1 red bell pepper
- ½ cup coriander, roughly chopped
- ¾ cup full-fat coconut milk

Instructions:

Heat a large skillet over medium heat. Once the oil is hot, add the mustard and cumin seeds. Stir frequently for 1 minute until the seeds become fragrant and start to bounce around the pan. Add the chopped onion and sauté for 3-4 minutes until soft, then add the garlic and ginger.

Mix in all the spices and allow them to roast on the pan for a minute, stirring constantly, then remove from the heat.

In a high-speed blender, transfer all the sauté ingredients along with the tomatoes, pepper, coriander, and coconut milk. Blend until smooth and creamy.

Carefully pour the sauce ingredients back into the skillet (no need to wash it), and bring the sauce to a simmer before adding the cauliflower florets. Cook within 10 minutes, then remove the lid, give the mixture a good stir and cook for a further 10 minutes uncovered for the curry to reduce and thicken.

Taste for seasoning and serve with rice or naan bread.

23. Teriyaki Salmon with Garlic Butter Asparagus

Fattening up the salmon strips to a medium steak-like consistency is about as difficult as it sounds. A few minutes of grill time does the trick. Getting a buttery garlic teriyaki dressing, however, requires a little more time and patience – but well worth it. The best part? You can make this dish in less than 30 minutes and share it with anyone for dinner!

Serving size: 4

Cooking time: 20 minutes

Ingredients:

For the salmon

- ⅓ cup mirin (Japanese sweet rice wine)
- ½ cup gluten-free soy sauce or coconut aminos
- 2 tablespoons coconut sugar
- 2 tablespoons freshly squeezed lime juice
- 2 teaspoons toasted sesame oil
- 3 garlic cloves, minced
- 1 (1-inch) piece fresh ginger, minced
- 4 (6-ounce) skin-on salmon fillets
- 2 tablespoons non-dairy butter

For the asparagus

- 2 tablespoons non-dairy butter
- 2 garlic cloves, minced
- 1-pound asparagus, trimmed
- 1 teaspoon grated lemon zest
- Salt
- Freshly ground black pepper

Instructions:

To make the salmon

In a baking dish, mix the mirin, soy sauce, coconut sugar, lime juice, oil, garlic, then the ginger. Place the salmon skin-side up in the sauce. Cover and refrigerate for at least 30 minutes but no longer than 1 hour.

Preheat the oven to 425°F.

In a large ovenproof skillet, heat the butter over medium-high heat. Swirl the butter to coat the skillet. Remove the salmon from the marinade, reserving the marinade. Put the salmon in the skillet, skin-side up0—Cook for 2 minutes. Flip the salmon and spoon ½ cup of the marinade on top.

Place the skillet in the oven and roast for 8 minutes, or until browned and the fish is opaque.

To make the asparagus

In a skillet over medium heat, melt the butter. Put the garlic and cook, stirring, for 1 minute. Add the asparagus and cook, turning often, for 8 minutes or until tender-crisp.

Sprinkle with the lemon zest. If desired, add salt and pepper to taste. Serve with the salmon.

24. Tuna Salad Stuffed Tomatoes

Tuna salad stuffed tomatoes are a wholesome dinner side dish that will keep you feeling satisfied all day long.

Full of healthy fats and packed with protein, these tuna stuffed tomatoes can be whipped up in minutes and will taste like you spent hours at the stove.

Serving size: 4

Cooking time: 0 minutes

Ingredients:

- 4 large beefsteak tomatoes
- 2 (5-ounce) cans albacore tuna
- ½ cup finely diced celery
- ⅓ cup vegan mayonnaise
- ¼ cup minced onion
- 1 tablespoon yellow mustard
- 1 tablespoon chopped fresh dill
- 2 teaspoons freshly squeezed lemon juice
- ¼ teaspoon salt
- ¼ teaspoon ground white pepper
- Paprika, for garnish

Instructions:

Chop the tops off the tomatoes and reserve. With a spoon, scoop out the insides and the seeds, like you would when carving a pumpkin. Set aside.

Mix the tuna, celery, mayonnaise, onion, mustard, dill, lemon juice, salt, and pepper in a bowl.

Spoon the tuna mixture into the tomatoes, dividing evenly. Garnish with extra dill and a sprinkle of paprika.

Set the reserved tomato tops on top like little hats.

25. Pesto Salmon with Asparagus

This dish is a perfect dinner option for a Friday night. Salmon and asparagus are both great sources of protein, so it's filling without being too heavy.

Serving size: 3

Cooking time: 15 minutes

Ingredients:

- 1 tablespoon extra-virgin olive oil
- 1 bunch asparagus, woody ends trimmed
- Sea salt to taste
- Black pepper, freshly ground
- 1½ pounds salmon, ideally one thick fillet
- ¼ cup prepared pesto

Instructions:

Preheat your oven to 375°F.

Line the baking sheet with parchment paper.

Cover the asparagus with olive oil, then season generously with pepper and salt. Spread the asparagus spears out on the prepped baking sheet, leaving space in the center of the pan for the salmon.

Coat the salmon with the pesto and place it on the pan in the center.

Roast, uncovered, for 15 minutes, until the salmon is not quite cooked through; it should still be deep pink in the center, but flake with a fork. It will continue cooking after it emerges from the oven.

26. Fish and Chips

Fish and chips is a dish consisting of fried pieces of salted, dried, and sometimes breaded fish, usually most commonly cod or haddock, with fries. It is often garnished with salt or vinegar.

Serving size: 4

Cooking time: 25 minutes

Ingredients:

- 2 large Russet potatoes
- 2 tablespoons extra-virgin olive oil
- ½ teaspoon sea salt, divided
- 1½ cups gluten-free bread crumbs
- ¼ teaspoon garlic powder
- Pinch cayenne pepper
- 2 eggs
- 1½ pounds cod fillets, cut into 1-inch-thick spears

Instructions:

Preheat the oven to 425°F.

Arrange the baking sheet with parchment paper.

Spread the potato spears on the pan and drizzle with olive oil. Gently toss to coat. Season with ¼ teaspoon of salt. Bake for 15 minutes.

Meanwhile, mix the bread crumbs, the remaining ¼ teaspoon salt, garlic powder, and cayenne pepper in a shallow dish.

Thoroughly whisk the eggs in a separate shallow dish.

Dip the cod fillets into the seasoned bread crumbs mixture, then dip them into the egg, and then dip, once more, into the bread crumbs.

Transfer the potatoes from the oven and add the coated fish to the pan—Bake for 10 minutes more, or until the fish is cooked through and the potatoes are browned.

27. Baja Fish Tacos

These tacos are a truly Mexican delight. They use a flour tortilla in the traditional taco-using fashion, topped with a zesty slaw, spicy sauce, and crunchy cabbage. The dish is versatile in that you can add just about any protein to the mix! Try adding grilled shrimp or avocado for an extra kick to your taste buds!

Serving size: 8

Cooking time: 15 minutes

Ingredients:

- 2 tablespoons extra-virgin olive oil
- Zest of 1 lime
- Juice of 1 lime
- 1 teaspoon ground cumin
- ⅛ teaspoon cayenne pepper
- 1 teaspoon ancho Chile powder
- ¼ teaspoon sea salt
- 1-pound mahi-mahi, cut into 4-inch-long pieces
- ½ cup mayonnaise
- ½ cup sour cream
- ¼ cup minced fresh cilantro
- 16 gluten-free corn tortillas
- 1 cup shredded cabbage
- ½ red onion, thinly sliced
- 1 cup store-bought gluten-free roasted tomato salsa

Instructions:

In a large, nonreactive dish, whisk the olive oil, lime zest, lime juice, cumin, ancho Chile powder, salt, and cayenne pepper. Add the mahi-mahi to this mixture, turn to coat, and refrigerate for 10 minutes.

In a small jar, whisk the mayonnaise, sour cream, and cilantro. Cover and refrigerate until ready to serve.

Warm a sauté pan over medium-high heat until hot. Remove the mahi-mahi from the marinade, add to the skillet, and panfry for 3 to 4 minutes on each side, or until it flakes easily with a fork.

Evenly divide the fish among the tortillas. Top each taco with some of the shredded cabbage, onion, and salsa. Finish with a dollop of the cilantro sauce.

28. Coconut-Crusted Shrimp

This low-carb, gluten-free dinner will keep you satisfied for days. And, if you don't think about what the shrimp was dipped in before cooking it well, that's your fault. These shrimp are crispy and flavorful on the outside with a creamy coconut center.

Serving size: 4

Cooking time: 5 minutes

Ingredients:

- ¼ cup Whole-Grain Gluten-Free Flour Blend
- 1½ cups unsweetened shredded coconut
- 2 egg whites
- ½ teaspoon sea salt
- ¼ teaspoon garlic powder
- 1½ pounds jumbo shrimp, peeled and butterflied
- ¼ cup coconut oil

Instructions:

Place the flour blend in a small bowl.

Place the coconut in another small bowl.

In a third small bowl, whisk the egg whites, salt, and garlic powder.

Dip each shrimp into the flour blend, then the egg white mixture, and then dredge in the coconut. Place each on a plate.

Warm sauté pans over medium-high heat until hot, about 2 minutes.

Melt the coconut oil in the skillet and tilt the pan to coat the bottom.

When the oil is hot, transfer the shrimp to the pan and cook for 2 to 3 minutes on each side until golden brown, crisp, and cooked through.

29. Ginger Veggie Stir-Fry

This simple vegetarian dish is as flavorful as it is easy to prepare. Load up your favorite skillet with stir-fry vegetables, garlic, and ginger, then add a bit of soy sauce and sugar. Once they're cooked down to perfection, they'll be ready for you to mix in rice noodles and serve! Whether it's a Saturday night or a busy weeknight, this dish will help you satisfy your hunger without breaking the bank.

Serving size: 3

Cooking time: 17 minutes

Ingredients:

- 3 tablespoons sesame oil or vegetable oil
- 2 (14-ounce) packages extra-firm tofu, drained, pressed, and cut into ¾-inch cubes
- 3 tablespoons tamari, divided
- ½ cup finely chopped onion
- 2 tablespoons minced garlic
- 1 tablespoon ginger
- 1 to 2 teaspoons chili paste
- 1 cup chopped fresh broccoli florets
- ½ cup shredded carrots
- ½ cup chopped red bell pepper
- ½ cup chopped green bell pepper
- ½ cup fresh sugar snap peas

Instructions:

Warm the oil over medium-high heat. Once hot, add the tofu and 1 tablespoon tamari. Sauté, stirring occasionally, until the tofu is lightly colored, about 8 minutes. Add the onion, garlic, ginger, chili paste, and the remaining 2 tablespoons tamari. Stir and cook until fragrant, about 1 minute.

Add the broccoli, carrots, bell peppers, and peas. Sauté for 5 to 8 minutes, until cooked but still crisp.

Serve hot with your preferred grain brown rice, quinoa, gluten-free noodles, or cauliflower rice, along with additional tamari to taste.

30. Simple Spaghetti Squash Bake

Spaghetti squash is a pure winter treat. But, once you take it from the freezer, you'll find that it's as hard as a rock. In order to make this delicacy that much more tender and delicious, we have a simple spaghetti squash bake recipe that uses just six ingredients and takes less than 25 minutes! Try out the delicious recipe below for an easy dinner on those rushed days or as a first course before a major holiday meal.

Serving size: 6

Cooking time: 55 minutes

Ingredients:

- 1 spaghetti squash
- ½ cup water
- 2 tablespoons extra-virgin olive oil
- ½ red bell pepper, chopped
- ½ green bell pepper, chopped
- ⅓ red onion, chopped
- 2 tablespoons minced garlic
- 1 (32-ounce) can crushed tomatoes
- ¼ cup chopped fresh basil
- Salt
- Freshly ground black pepper
- 1 cup ricotta cheese
- 1 cup shredded mozzarella

Instructions:

Preheat the oven to 400°F.

Carefully remove the ends of spaghetti squash and cut in half lengthwise. Place in a microwave-safe bowl with the water. Microwave for 20 minutes or until soft. Carefully remove from the microwave and let stand until cool enough to handle. Remove the seeds. Scoop the flesh from the shell and place it in an 8-inch square baking dish.

In a sauté pan or skillet, heat the olive oil over medium-high heat. Sauté the peppers, onion, and garlic. Cook until fragrant, about 3 minutes. Put the tomatoes and basil and season with salt and pepper. Simmer for about 15 minutes until slightly reduced and thickened.

Pour the tomato mixture over the spaghetti squash—layer the ricotta cheese and mozzarella over the top.

Bake for 35 minutes, until golden.

31. Rainbow Grain Bowl

Tired of the same old boring grain bowl? Well, we've got just what you need: a rainbow grain bowl. It's as colorful as it is nutritious and easy to make, so you can enjoy it for dinner. I hope this dish brightens your day!

Serving size: 6

Cooking time: 0 minutes

Ingredients:

- 2 cups cooked quinoa or rice
- 2 cups cooked chickpeas or lentils
- 1½ cups corn kernels
- 1½ cups sliced cherry tomatoes
- 1½ cups sliced cucumbers
- 1½ cups snap peas
- 2 avocados, halved, pitted, and sliced
- ¾ cup chopped fresh basil
- 6 tablespoons nuts or seeds (sesame seeds, pumpkin seeds, almonds, cashews, or pecans)
- 2 tablespoons garlic powder
- ¾ cup Greek Yogurt Ranch Dip, for serving

Instructions:

In six bowls, divide the quinoa, chickpeas, corn, tomatoes, cucumbers, and peas. Add a few avocado slices, sprinkle with basil, nuts, and garlic powder, and drizzle with ranch dressing.

Grain bowls are great to assemble in advance because none of the vegetables get soggy like a traditional salad. Simply assemble in airtight containers and store in the refrigerator for 3 to 5 days for easy grab-and-go meals.

For best results, keep the avocado and ranch separate until ready to serve.

32. Southern Rice and Beans

Southern rice and beans is the perfect example of the type of dish that is often called comfort food, as it provides a way to remember home and family more than any other dish. It's packed with flavor, has lots of vegetables, and it just tastes great. It doesn't have to be served on New Year's Day or Thanksgiving, but during these days, when you're looking for something that will remind you of home or your loved ones who are not there with you at this time.

Serving size: 4

Cooking time: 19 minutes

Ingredients:

- 1 cup long-grain rice
- 2 tablespoons extra-virgin olive oil
- 1 onion, finely chopped
- 1 red bell pepper, chopped
- 1 green bell pepper, chopped
- 2 medium tomatoes, seeded and chopped
- 1 dried chipotle chili, finely chopped
- 1 cup canned red kidney beans
- 1 tablespoon fresh basil, chopped
- 2 teaspoons fresh thyme, chopped
- 1 teaspoon Homemade Cajun Seasoning
- Pinch salt
- Freshly ground black pepper
- Fresh basil leaves, for garnish

Instructions:

Cook the rice in salted water for about 12 minutes. Transfer to a large bowl and set aside.

Heat the oil in a skillet. Put the onion and bell peppers and cook for 5 minutes until soft. Stir in the tomatoes and chili and cook for another 2 minutes.

Add the vegetable mixture and kidney beans to the cooked rice and gently combine.

Add the herbs and the Homemade Cajun Seasoning to the rice and stir to combine.

Put salt and pepper, and garnish with fresh basil.

33. Veggie and Pineapple Fried Rice

Veggie and Pineapple Fried Rice is a delicious and healthy dinner recipe that is even better the next day. The best part? It's easy to make, and it can be prepared in a few minutes. So, grab your ingredients and get cooking!

Serving size: 4

Cooking time: 13 minutes

Ingredients:

- 2 cups uncooked white rice or 5 to 6 cups leftover rice
- 4 tablespoons butter, divided
- 1 medium onion, chopped
- 3 large carrots, peeled and chopped
- 4 small zucchinis, chopped
- Salt
- Freshly ground black pepper
- 5 garlic cloves, minced
- 1 cup pineapple chunks
- 5 tablespoons tamari or gluten-free soy sauce
- 1 tablespoon sesame oil
- 1 bunch scallion

Instructions:

Set the rice to cook.

Heat a large cast-iron pan over medium heat. Add 2 tablespoons of butter and sauté the onion for 3 to 4 minutes, or until it starts to brown.

Add the carrots and cook for 2 minutes, then add the zucchini—Cook for 3 minutes, or until the vegetables are tender. Put salt and pepper and set aside.

Warm a wok within medium heat, then put the rest 2 tablespoons of butter. Sauté the garlic for 1 minute.

Add the rice and pineapple to the wok. Using a metal spatula, make sure you get to the bottom of the pan and gently incorporate the rice and garlic.

Stir in the vegetable mixture, then add the tamari and sesame oil and cook for 3 more minutes. Put salt and pepper, then garnish with the scallions before serving.

34. Beef Tacos

Do you love the taste of tacos but are looking for something different? Look no further! You might be surprised to know that beef tacos are delicious, easy to make, and portable. They are perfect for a quick dinner or for taking out on the road with friends and family.

Serving size: 4

Cooking time: 20 minutes

Ingredients:

- 4 corn tortillas
- 1 tablespoon olive oil
- 9 ounces extra-lean ground beef
- 1 leek
- 1 teaspoon ground cumin
- 1 teaspoon ground coriander
- ½ teaspoon sea salt
- ½ avocado, chopped
- ½ cup grated Cheddar cheese
- ¼ cup Fat-free yogurt or sour cream

Instructions:

Preheat the oven to 350°F. Cover the tortillas in aluminum foil, then heat in the oven for 15 minutes.

Meanwhile, heat a large nonstick skillet over medium-high heat and add the olive oil.

Add the ground beef, leek, cumin, coriander, and salt. Cook, crumbling the ground beef with a spoon until it is browned for about 5 minutes.

To assemble the tacos, portion the beef on the tortillas. Top with avocado, Cheddar, and sour cream. Enjoy!

35. Ground Lamb and Lentils

Lentils and ground lamb are great for a minimalist meal. They can be prepared in a variety of ways, such as served over salad, tossed with rice and vegetables, or served on their own with bread.

Serving size: 5

Cooking time: 10 minutes

Ingredients:

- 12 ounces Extra-lean ground lamb
- 1 leek, green part only, chopped and washed
- 2 cups canned lentils
- 1 cup Poultry Broth
- 1 tablespoon ground cumin
- 1 teaspoon ground coriander
- ½ teaspoon sea salt
- 1 teaspoon grated lime zest
- ¼ cup fresh cilantro, chopped

Instructions:

Heat a large pot over medium-high heat. Cook the ground lamb and leek, crumbling the meat with a spoon until it is browned for about 5 minutes.

Add the lentils, broth, cumin, coriander, and salt. Cook, occasionally stirring, for 5 more minutes.

Serve garnished with lime zest and cilantro.

36. Herb-Crusted Lamb Chops

What makes these herb-crusted lamb chops so special? Well, for one thing, they're incredibly easy to make! They only take a few minutes to cook and come with a lemon butter sauce that's quick and delicious. Plus, the lamb is organic and humanely raised, which means it's extra tender, and the thyme leaves a light flavor on your chops.

Serving size: 2

Cooking time: 10 minutes

Ingredients:

- ¾ cup gluten-free breadcrumbs
- 1 tablespoon unsalted grass-fed butter, at room temperature
- 1 teaspoon Dijon mustard
- ¼ cup fresh rosemary leaves
- ¼ cup fresh oregano leaves
- ¼ cup fresh parsley
- ½ teaspoon sea salt
- 4 extra-lean lamb loin chops

Instructions:

Preheat your oven to 325°F.

Pulse in the food processor the breadcrumbs, butter, mustard, rosemary, oregano, parsley, and salt 20 times, or until the herbs are chopped and well combined with the breadcrumbs.

Spread the mixture on the lamb chops, pressing so it sticks to the surface of the meat.

In a large nonstick skillet, add the chops. Brown them for 3 minutes per side, then transfer them to a rimmed baking sheet.

Bake for 6 minutes or until the lamb reaches an internal temperature of 145°F. Serve.

37. Open-Faced Stuffed Burgers

These burgers have a plethora of great flavors in them. No need to wait until you have a grill this summer; with these, you can enjoy your favorite burgers year-round!

In addition, these burgers are made from 100% ground beef! The meat is mixed with bread crumbs, onions, eggs, salt, and pepper that are then shaped into thin patties.

Serving size: 4

Cooking time: 10 minutes

Ingredients:

- ½ cup lactose-free nonfat milk
- ¼ cup gluten-free breadcrumbs
- 1 pound extra-lean ground beef
- ½ teaspoon sea salt
- 1 teaspoon Dijon mustard
- ½ teaspoon fish sauce
- ½ cup grated Cheddar cheese
- 4 tablespoons Freshly chopped basil
- 4 slices gluten-free bread, toasted
- 4 tablespoons Healthy Burger Sauce

Instructions:

Mix the milk and breadcrumbs. Allow it to rest for 10 minutes.

Mix the ground beef, breadcrumb mixture, salt, mustard, and fish sauce until well mixed. Roll into eight balls and pat each out into a ¼-inch thick patty.

In a small bowl, mix the cheese and basil. Sprinkle the cheese mixture on each of the four patties and top with another patty. Pinch the edges to seal.

Preheat a nonstick skillet on medium-high. Put the burger patties in the pot and heat until cooked, about 5 minutes per side.

Serve on the toasted bread with 1 tablespoon of the Healthy Burger Sauce spooned over the top of each.

38. Easy Beef Biryani

This dish is popular in countries like India and Pakistan. It's a Pakistani version of Indian Biryani, which is a long-grain rice dish coated with clarified butter and spices before cooking. Beef or lamb can be substituted with chicken or vegetables if you prefer something less spicy. You will need to make sure that your beef or lamb, however, is already partially cooked, so the end result will not be raw. Serve this delicious dish with cucumber raita and a side of mint chutney.

Serving size: 6

Cooking time: 15 minutes

Ingredients:

- 1 medium yellow onion, peeled and sliced
- 1-pound top round, cut into 1/2" strips
- 1/4 cup golden raisins
- 1 tablespoon minced fresh ginger
- 2 cloves garlic, peeled and minced
- 1/2 teaspoon ground cloves
- 1/2 teaspoon ground cardamom
- 1/2 teaspoon ground coriander
- 1/2 teaspoon ground black pepper
- 1/2 teaspoon cinnamon
- 1/2 teaspoon ground cumin
- 1 tablespoon ghee or unsalted butter
- 1 teaspoon salt
- 1 cup plain full-fat yogurt
- 1 (28-ounce) can whole stewed tomatoes, including juice
- 2 cups cooked basmati rice
- 1/4 cup chopped fresh mint leaves

Instructions:

Warm ghee 30 seconds. Add onion to the pot and sauté 5 minutes until onions are browned and starting to caramelize. Add all remaining ingredients except rice and mint to the pot.

Adjust cooking time to 10 minutes. Transfer into six bowls over cooked basmati rice.

Garnish with mint leaves and serve warm.

39. Quick Beef and Broccoli

If you're looking for a delicious and healthy dinner, you'll want to try beef and broccoli stir fry. This dish is quick, simple, and full of flavor. It's also very versatile to use different vegetables as inspiration for your own stir fry! And it's a great way to use any leftover beef from the fridge.

So grab some veggies and put them in the pan with some beef and water or broth.

Serving size: 2

Cooking time: 6 minutes

Ingredients:

Sauce

- 2 cloves garlic, peeled and minced
- 1/3 cup tamari
- 1/4 cup rice wine vinegar
- 2 tablespoons honey
- 1 tablespoon sesame oil
- 1/4 teaspoon ground ginger
- 1/4 teaspoon salt
- 1/8 teaspoon cayenne pepper

Beef & Broccoli

- 1 medium head broccoli
- 1 (1-pound) boneless sirloin
- 1 cup water

Instructions:

Mix sauce fixing. Set aside 2 tablespoons of sauce. Put the beef in the bowl and toss. Refrigerate within 30 minutes.

Warm the pot within 2 minutes. Put meat in a pot and stir-fry 2 minutes. Next is the broccoli, and toss 1 minute. Place beef and broccoli in a large bowl.

Pour water into the Instant Pot. Insert steamer basket. Add beef and broccoli to the basket. Adjust cooking time to 1 minute.

Serve with the rest of the sauce.

40. Greek Lamb-Stuffed Eggplants

This Greek-inspired dish is a wonderful main course, suitable for a dinner party. The eggplants are filled with ground lamb and pine nuts and then baked in the oven until they get crispy on top. Finally, they're drizzled with lemon juice and olive oil before serving. This dish is also vegan if you use soy crumbles instead of ground lamb or just omit it entirely.

Serving size: 4

Cooking time: 10 minutes

Ingredients:

- 8 small eggplants, about 4 to 5 inches in length
- ½ cup olive oil
- ½ cup minced onion
- 4 cloves garlic, minced
- ½ pound lean ground lamb
- Salt and pepper to taste
- ½ cup fresh tomato, finely chopped
- 3 tablespoons chopped fresh mint
- ¼ teaspoon ground coriander Juice of ½ lemon

For garnish:

- Yogurt, extra mint leaves, and finely chopped tomato

Instructions:

Fry the whole eggplants in olive oil. Once cool down, make a slit from top to bottom but do not cut through.

Over moderate heat, fry the onion, garlic, lamb, salt, pepper, tomato, and herbs. Moisten with lemon juice.

Stir well while breaking the lamb. Set aside to cool for 15 minutes. Put the eggplants on a baking sheet that has been covered with aluminum foil. Spread the eggplants open and fill with lamb stuffing.

Preheat oven to 400°F.

Bake for 10 minutes. Arrange with a dollop of yogurt on each eggplant and garnish with mint and chopped tomato. Serve.

41. Stuffed Pork Chops

Pork chops stuffed with cheese and spinach are a fantastically simple dish that will appeal to all the meat-eaters in your life. And while they're a little more work than simply throwing a steak on the grill, they'll taste even better - especially when served alongside mashed potatoes and sautéed green beans.

Serving size: 4

Cooking time: 40 minutes

Ingredients:

- 1 tart apple, peeled, cored, and chopped
- ½ cup chopped onion
- 1 tablespoon dried rosemary, crumbled
- ¼ cup finely chopped Italian flat-leaf parsley
- ½ cup olive oil
- ½ cup gluten-free cornbread crumbs
- Salt and pepper to taste
- 4 thick-cut pork rib chops
- ¼ cup olive oil
- 4 garlic cloves, chopped
- 2 onions, chopped
- ½ cup chicken broth
- ½ cup dry white wine
- Zest and juice of ½ lemon
- 2 ripe pears, peeled, cored, and quartered
- 2 teaspoons cornstarch mixed with 2 ounces cold water (to thicken the gravy)

Instructions:

Sauté the apple, onion, and herbs in ½ cup olive oil. When softened, add the cornbread crumbs, salt, and pepper. When cool enough to handle, stuff into the chops and secure with toothpicks.

Add ¼ cup olive oil to the pan and brown the chops on medium-high. Add the rest of the fixing, except for the cornstarch-and-water mixture, and cover. Simmer for 40 minutes over very low heat.

Place the chops on a warm platter and add the cornstarch-and-water mixture to the gravy in the pan if you want it to be thicker. Add salt and pepper to taste.

42. Burger and Veggie Bowls

Summer is the best time of year for outdoor family get-togethers, and what's better than burgers on the grill? This recipe for veggie burger bowls is a healthy alternative to a greasy patty with all the fixings. You'll use your favorite veggies, put them in a bowl or on a plate, and top with a hearty, flavorful tomato sauce with pesto added. It's not only easy but also delicious!

Serving size: 4

Cooking time: 20 minutes

Ingredients:

For the Burgers:

- 1-pound ground beef
- 1 teaspoon garlic powder
- 1 teaspoon salt
- ½ teaspoon ground black pepper
- ½ teaspoon paprika
- 1 teaspoon dried thyme
- 2 tablespoons olive oil
- 1 egg

For the Vegetables:

- 2 zucchinis, sliced
- 1 medium butternut squash, peeled, diced
- 2 cups cherry tomatoes halves
- ½ teaspoon salt
- ¼ teaspoon ground black pepper
- 4 tablespoons olive oil

Instructions:

Switch on the oven, then set it to 425 degrees F, and let it preheat.

Take a baking sheet, place zucchini and butternut squash on it, season with salt and black pepper, toss until well coated roasted for 15 minutes until vegetables are tender.

Meanwhile, prepare the burger and for this, place all its ingredients in a bowl, mix well and then shape into four thick patties.

Take a grill pan, place it over medium heat, grease it with oil, and when hot, add patties and cook for 5 minutes per side until thoroughly cooked.

Let the vegetables and patties cool, then portion them evenly between four heatproof glass meal prep containers and tighten with lid.

When ready to eat, thaw the burgers and vegetables and then reheat in the microwave oven until hot.

Serve with cherry tomatoes.

43. Chili Beef Pasta

This quick and easy recipe will satisfy your craving for a hearty meal in no time. There is nothing better than something that tastes great, is easy to make in large batches, and can be customized in dozens of ways to suit any taste. Try marinating the beef with red pepper flakes, oregano, cumin, or garlic powder before cooking it for authentic flavor. For a vegetarian pasta dish, try using fresh spinach instead of meat.

Serving size: 4

Cooking time: 28 minutes

Ingredients:

- 8 ounces spiral pasta, gluten-free, uncooked
- 1-pound ground beef
- 2 tablespoons minced onion, dried
- 1/2 teaspoon garlic powder
- 2 teaspoons red chili powder
- 2 teaspoons dried oregano
- 1 teaspoon sugar
- 1/8 teaspoon salt
- 6 ounces tomato paste
- 2 cups water
- 3 cups tomato juice

Instructions:

Take a large saucepan, place it over medium heat and when hot, add beef and cook for 8 minutes until beef is no longer pink.

Drain, then put remaining ingredients except for pasta, stir well and bring the mixture to boil.

Then reduce heat to medium-low level, add pasta and simmer for 20 minutes until pasta is tender, covering the pan.

Remove the saucepan from heat, let the pasta cool completely and then portion it evenly between four heatproof glass meal prep containers.

Tighten the containers with a lid and store them in the freezer for up to one month.

When ready to eat, thaw the pasta, then reheat in the microwave oven until hot and serve.

44. Beef Ragu Pasta

It's perfect for when you want something hearty and warming like a stew but don't want to make the time commitment of an all-day slow cooking process.

Serving size: 8

Cooking time: 9 hours

Ingredients:

- 28 ounces crushed tomatoes
- 1 ½ pounds sirloin roast
- 1 medium white onion, peeled, chopped
- 2 medium carrots, peeled, chopped
- 1 teaspoon sliced garlic
- 1 teaspoon ground black pepper
- 1 ½ teaspoons salt
- 1 teaspoon dried thyme
- 3 dried bay leaves
- 1 tablespoon olive oil
- 1 cup beef broth
- 1-pound pasta, gluten-free, uncooked

Instructions:

Coat roast with oil, then season with salt and black pepper on both sides and rub the seasonings into the meat for 1 minute.

Then place steaks into a slow cooker, top with tomatoes, add onion, carrots, garlic, thyme, bay leaf and pour in broth.

Switch on the slow cooker, shut it with lid and cook for 6 hours at high heat setting or 9 hours at low heat setting.

Meanwhile, prepare the pasta and for this, place a pot over medium heat half-full with water and bring it to a boil.

Followed by pasta, set for 10 minutes until tender, then drain it and set aside until required.

When done, remove bay leaf, shred the beef, stir well and let cool completely.

Portion beef evenly between eight heatproof glass meal prep containers, add pasta, then tighten the containers with lid and store in the freezer for up to one month.

When ready to eat, thaw the beef and pasta, then reheat in the microwave oven until hot and serve.

45. Masala Green Beans

Masala Green Beans is an easy recipe that you'll love to make over and over again! If you like fresh, light green beans, then this dish will be your new favorite. It's hearty and filling enough to make a meal out of! Crispy fried onion and ginger add depth and flavor to buttery green beans coated in a spiced tomato sauce.

Serving size: 4

Cooking time: 20 minutes

Ingredients:

- 75g onion
- 3 large cloves garlic, finely chopped
- 1 teaspoon ground cumin
- 1 teaspoon ground coriander
- 1 teaspoon sweet paprika
- ½ teaspoon red chili pepper flakes
- ¾ teaspoon salt
- 180ml coconut milk
- 2-kilo green beans
- Juice of ½ a lime
- 2 tablespoons cilantro, chopped

Instructions:

Sauté spices until fragrant, then put aside.

Warm up the oil in the pan, then put onion and garlic, cook until soft and turn light brown.

Add toasted spices, coconut milk, and green beans, reduce heat and simmer gently for 15-20 minutes until beans are tender. Squeeze fresh lime juice on beans and garnish with fresh cilantro.

46. Potato with Cauliflower

If you're looking for a healthy, filling meal with plenty of vegetables, this dish is for you! Simply roast sweet potatoes and cauliflower in the oven until golden brown and tender, toss them together with olive oil and salt, then top with fresh parsley.

Serving size: 3

Cooking time: 15 minutes

Ingredients:

- 1 cauliflower, cut into small florets
- 1 russet potato
- 2 tablespoons ginger
- 2 tablespoons garlic
- 1 tablespoon ground coriander
- ¼ teaspoon turmeric
- 240ml coconut milk, divided
- 2 tablespoons oil
- 1 large Serrano pepper
- 1 teaspoon cumin seeds
- Salt
- 2 tablespoons cilantro leaves

Instructions:

Blend the ginger, garlic, coriander, turmeric, and 125ml coconut milk in a blender to make a wet masala, set aside.

Put oil, Serrano pepper, wait 30 seconds, and then add the cumin seeds in a large pot and wait until it is finished spluttering. Carefully add the wet masala.

Add the cauliflower and potatoes, Season with salt and add the remainder of the coconut milk. Set to cook within medium heat 10 to 15 minutes.

Garnish with cilantro and serve immediately.

47. Carrots Peas & Potatoes

If you're looking for a way to get your veggies in, look no further. This is not a garden-variety recipe - this dish is packed with veggies and flavor! Carrots, peas, and potatoes combine for a healthy dinner that will satisfy the fussiest of eaters.

Serving size: 5

Cooking time: 20 minutes

Ingredients:

- 1 packet of frozen mixed peas and carrots
- 4 potatoes, diced
- 1 onion, chopped
- 1 tablespoon ground cumin
- 1 teaspoon ground turmeric
- 1 tablespoon ground coriander
- 1 teaspoon chili powder
- ½ teaspoon salt
- 1 tablespoon oil
- 120ml water

Instructions:

Put oil, onion, cumin, turmeric, coriander, chili powder, and salt, cook in a large pot.

Decrease to the medium setting, then stir in the potatoes, carrots, and peas, add water as needed. Stir well, then cover and cook until potatoes are tender for about 20 minutes.

48. Paprika Spiced Turkey

This year, don't forget to spice up Thanksgiving by adding a new delicious meal - Paprika Spiced Turkey. It's easy, adaptable, and will make your holiday meal the one to remember.

Not only is this side dish the perfect complement to the traditional turkey, mashed potatoes, and cranberry sauce, but it's also a delicious alternative for those looking for a gluten-free or paleo diet.

Serving size: 6

Cooking time: 54 minutes

Ingredients:

- 8 cloves garlic minced
- 2 tablespoons smoked paprika
- ½ teaspoon red pepper flakes
- 1-pound turkey thighs
- ½ cup olive oil
- ½ teaspoon salt
- ½ teaspoon black pepper
- ½ cup water
- ¼ cup parsley, chopped
- 2 tablespoons oregano, chopped

Instructions:

Take your Instant Pot and place it over a dry kitchen platform.

Open the lid and select the "Sauté" cooking function.

Add the oil, garlic, smoked paprika, herbs, and red pepper flakes into the pot; cook for 1 minute to soften the garlic.

Season the turkey and add to the pot, cover in the garlic mix, and brown for 2-3 minutes

Take out the turkey and set it aside.

Put the water into the pot, then stir with the herb mix, and then arrange the trivet in the pot.

Now place the turkey into the trivet.

Lock the top lid and make sure that the valve is sealed properly.

Select the "Manual" cooking function. Set the cooking time to 50 minutes.

Your Instant Pot will start building the pressure and begin the cooking cycle after a sufficient level of pressure is reached.

After the cooking time is over, press the "Cancel" setting, and then press "NPR" for natural release of the internal pressure. It takes around 10 minutes to release the pressure naturally.

Open the top lid and slice the turkey, top with the oregano and parsley; enjoy the recipe.

49. Lettuce Chicken Wraps

Lettuce Chicken Wraps is a light and refreshing hand-held meal that can be made in a few minutes. If you want to get fancy, top them with fresh mango salsa for a little extra zip.

What makes these wraps so good? Lettuce is part of the cabbage family which means it has lots of nutrients like fiber and antioxidants that will keep you healthy.

Serving size: 5

Cooking time: 15 minutes

Ingredients:

- 1 medium onion, minced
- 2 cups chicken broth
- 1 celery stalk
- 1 clove garlic
- 4-5 large lettuce leaves
- ½ cup buffalo wing sauce
- 1 large boneless, skinless chicken breast
- ½ cup shredded carrots

Instructions:

Take your Instant Pot and place it over a dry kitchen platform.

Open the lid and add the onions, garlic, chicken broth, sauce, and chicken. Stir the ingredients gently to combine with each other.

Lock the top lid and make sure that the valve is sealed properly.

Select "Poultry" cooking function. Set the cooking time to 15 minutes.

Your Instant Pot will start building the pressure and begin the cooking cycle after a sufficient level of pressure is reached.

After the cooking time is over, press the "Cancel" setting, and then press "NPR" for natural release of the internal pressure. It takes around 10 minutes to release the pressure naturally.

Open the top lid and shred the chicken.

Mix the chicken well with all the other ingredients.

Pour the chicken and sauce over the lettuce leaves.

Top with the shredded carrots and celery, then serve.

50. Herbed Chicken Rice

This dish is aromatic, satisfying, and filling. The chicken is lightly spiced with Greek seasonings and fried in olive oil. Rice cooked with onions, garlic, celery, carrots, tomatoes, white wine or chicken broth adds some substance to the more delicate herbs on top of the dish. A special touch of lemon zest at the end completes this lovely meal.

Serving size: 4

Cooking time: 15 minutes

Ingredients:

- 1 ½ cups long-grain rice
- 3 cups chicken broth
- 4 chicken breasts, halved
- 1 (8-ounce) package herb sprinkle of your choice
- 2 tablespoons oregano leaves
- Pepper and salt as per your taste preference

Instructions:

Season the chicken with the herbs of your choice. Set aside.

Take your Instant Pot and place it over a dry kitchen platform.

Open the lid and add the rice, chicken broth, pepper, salt, and oregano. Stir the ingredients gently to combine with each other.

Add the chicken and stir gently.

Lock the top lid and make sure that the valve is sealed properly.

Select "Poultry" cooking function. Set the cooking time to 15 minutes.

Your Instant Pot will start building the pressure and begin the cooking cycle after a sufficient level of pressure is reached.

After the cooking time is over, press the "Cancel" setting, and then press "QPR" to quickly release the internal pressure.

Open the top lid and transfer the rice to your serving bowls.

Serve and enjoy the recipe.

Conclusion

Thank you for reaching the end of this book. I hope you enjoyed the gluten-free recipes in this book.

No matter what your reason for following a gluten-free diet is, you should always consult with your doctor before changing your lifestyle and diet. As we said before, some people might find that they can safely consume small amounts of certain foods without adverse effects. This is because the severity of the reaction to gluten varies from person to person and can vary depending on many factors, such as weight and what medications one may be taking.

About the Author

Ivy's mission is to share her recipes with the world. Even though she is not a professional cook she has always had that flair toward cooking. Her hands create magic. She can make even the simplest recipe tastes superb. Everyone who has tried her food has astounding their compliments was what made her think about writing recipes.

She wanted everyone to have a taste of her creations aside from close family and friends. So, deciding to write recipes was her winning decision. She isn't interested in popularity, but how many people have her recipes reached and touched people. Each recipe in her cookbooks is special and has a special meaning in her life. This means that each recipe is created with attention and love. Every ingredient carefully picked, every combination tried and tested.

Her mission started on her birthday about 9 years ago, when her guests couldn't stop prizing the food on the table. The next thing she did was organizing an event where chefs from restaurants were tasting her recipes. This event gave her the courage to start spreading her recipes.

She has written many cookbooks and she is still working on more. There is no end in the art of cooking; all you need is inspiration, love, and dedication.

Author's Afterthoughts

I am thankful for downloading this book and taking the time to read it. I know that you have learned a lot and you had a great time reading it. Writing books is the best way to share the skills I have with your and the best tips too.

I know that there are many books and choosing my book is amazing. I am thankful that you stopped and took time to decide. You made a great decision and I am sure that you enjoyed it.

I will be even happier if you provide honest feedback about my book. Feedbacks helped by growing and they still do. They help me to choose better content and new ideas. So, maybe your feedback can trigger an idea for my next book.

Thank you again

Sincerely

Ivy Hope

Made in the USA
Columbia, SC
29 January 2024

f504fd64-5031-4ef1-b9c0-c7d61b71702eR01